ittle Mitchie

WHAT TO DO WHEN YOU FEEL SHY

MAKING NEW FRIENDS

ANNE ACCARDI

CREATING YOUNG NONFICTION READERS

Little Mitchie books spark curiosity and support early nonfiction reading for students in Grades 2-3. Designed to build vocabulary, support second language learners, and prepare readers for middle-grade content, each book includes helpful tips for parents and educators to build confidence and deepen understanding of the world.

TIPS FOR READING NONFICTION WITH BEGINNING READERS

Talk about Nonfiction

Begin by explaining that nonfiction books give us information that is true. The book will be organized around a specific topic or idea, and we may learn new facts through reading.

Look at the Parts

Most nonfiction books have helpful features. Our *Little Mitchie* titles include color photographs and graphic aids, a table of contents, a glossary, and an index. Share the purpose of these features with your reader.

Color Photos and Graphic Aids

A lot of information can be found by "reading" photos, charts, maps, and other graphic aids found within nonfiction texts. Help your reader learn more about the different ways information can be displayed.

Table of Contents

Located at the front of the book, this list shows the big ideas within the text and the page numbers where they can be found.

Glossary

Located at the back of the book, the glossary defines key words and phrases that are related to the topic. These words and phrases can be found in the text in colored type.

Index

Located at the back of the book, an index is an alphabetical list of topics and the page numbers where they can be found.

With a little help and guidance about reading nonfiction, you can feel good about introducing a young reader to the world of *Little Mitchie* nonfiction books.

Little Mitchie is an imprint of:

Mitchell Lane
PUBLISHERS

2001 SW 31st Avenue
Hallandale, FL 33009
mitchelllanepub.com

First Edition, 2027.

Author: Anne Accardi
Designer: Kathy Walsh
Editor: Kim Thompson

Library of Congress Cataloging-in-Publication Data
Title: What To Do When You Feel Shy / by Anne Accardi

Description: Hallandale, FL :
Mitchell Lane Publishers, [2027]

Identifiers:
ISBN 979-8-89260-901-2 (library bound)
ISBN 979-8-90145-058-1 (paperback)
ISBN 979-8-90145-005-5 (eBook)

Library of Congress Control Number: 2026930274

Photo credits: Shutterstock: Cover, p 1 & p 3 FREEPIK2; p 5, Anatoliy Karlyuk; p 6, Teerawat Anothaistaporn; p 9, PeopleImages; p 11 & 13, Ground Picture; p 14, EZ-Stock Studio; p 17 & 19, wavebreakmedia; p 21, Monkey Business Images

TABLE OF CONTENTS

Step One

KNOW THAT IT IS OKAY TO FEEL SHY

Do you ever feel **nervous** when meeting new people? Do you worry about **unfamiliar** places or events?

Everyone feels **shy** sometimes. Some people feel shy more often than others.

Feeling shy doesn't mean you want to be alone. It doesn't mean you don't want new friends. It just means you need a little time to warm up to new situations. That's okay!

Step Two

FACE YOUR FEARS

When you feel shy, talking to people might make you uncomfortable. You may be **self-conscious**. You might tremble, sweat, or get a stomachache.

It is normal to have these feelings. Go at your own **pace**. Don't rush. You'll soon feel more comfortable and **confident**.

FRIENDLY FACT

Breathing exercises can help. Take a deep breath in. Hold it for three seconds. Breathe out. Repeat until you feel calm.

Remember that friends are kind to each other. If someone is going to be your friend, they will be happy to talk to you!

It may help to have someone you trust at your side. Bring a friend, parent, or teacher with you when you talk to a new person.

CHALLENGE

Write three words that describe how you feel about a new person you meet. Do you feel curious, interested, or excited? Others feel the same way when they meet you!

Step Three

TAKE ACTION!

Go ahead and talk to someone you don't know well. Make **eye contact**. Use friendly **body language**. Smile, nod, and stand up straight. This will show you are happy to talk with them even if you feel shy.

FRIENDLY FACT

Smiling is a sign of friendliness across all countries, languages, and cultures.

Ask your new friend questions. You can ask about their hobbies, activities, or pets. Listen closely to their answers.

CHALLENGE

Write three questions you could ask a new friend.

After talking for a while, you will start to feel less shy. Try sharing something about yourself.

Invite your new friend to do something. Playing together is a great way to learn more about them.

Try these ways to invite someone to play with you.

- *I'm going to play ______ at recess. Would you like to do it too?*
- *What games are your favorite? Do you want to play one?*
- *I'd love to play ______ with you.*
- *What's your favorite thing to do at recess? Let's do that together.*

Step Four

KEEP GOING

Every time you talk to a new friend, it gets easier. You feel more comfortable. You don't feel so shy.

"When a shy person smiles, it's like the sun coming out."
—Anita Diamant

Keep talking to more people. Keep finding ways to **overcome** shyness. Soon, you will have lots of new friends!

TOP TIPS

Don't rush.

Bring someone you trust.

Take deep breaths.

Smile!

Make eye contact.

Ask questions.

GLOSSARY

body language (BAH-dee LANG-gwij) the thoughts and feelings your face and body communicate without using words

confident (KAHN-fi-duhnt) a strong belief in your own abilities; certain that things will happen in the way you expect

eye contact (eye KAHN-takt) looking at someone when speaking to them

nervous (NUR-vuhs) worried, scared, or anxious

overcome (oh-vur-KUHM) to defeat or deal with a problem

pace (pase) speed

self-conscious (self-KAHN-shuhs) constantly worried about how you look to other people and what they are thinking

shy (shye) uncomfortable around people you don't know well

unfamiliar (uhn-fuh-MIL-yur) new; unknown

Further Reading

Kim, Jaime. *Shy Robin and the First Day of School*. Candlewick, 2023.

Pearlstein, Howard. *The Shy Book*. Red Comet Press, 2026.

Spaeth, Katerina. *Shy Steve*. Paw Prints Publishing, 2024.

On the Internet

KidVision Feelings: Shy
youtube.com/watch?v=eCkzGvlqXS8
Watch a video to learn the signs of shyness and how to overcome them.

National Geographic Kids: How to Be an Awesome Friend
kids.nationalgeographic.com/pages/article/friend
Learn tips for making and keeping friends.

Index